THE
Archive Photographs
SERIES
SALISBURY PLAIN

THE SIDE WALK NEAR SHREWTON LODGE AT THE TIME OF THE FIRST WORLD WAR.

THE
Archive Photographs
SERIES

SALISBURY PLAIN

Compiled by
Peter Daniels and Rex Sawyer

CHALFORD

First published 1996
Copyright © Peter Daniels and Rex Sawyer, 1996

The Chalford Publishing Company
St Mary's Mill, Chalford,
Stroud, Gloucestershire, GL6 8NX

ISBN 0 7524 0754 6

Typesetting and origination by
The Chalford Publishing Company
Printed in Great Britain by
Redwood Books, Trowbridge

A SOUVENIR OF THE GREAT WAR FROM THE WILTSHIRE REGIMENT. Large numbers of postcards such as this were produced for the soldiers to keep in touch with their family and friends. This particular one was designed by Rattle and Company of Portsmouth. It records the campaigns of the 7th Battalion, Duke of Edinburgh's Wiltshire Regiment, from 4 August 1914 to 11 November 1918.

Contents

'VIRTUAL REALITY.' Peter Daniels and Rex Sawyer are pictured here with an 18-pounder QF Mark II field gun of 1918. Introduced in 1904, this quick-firing gun was the most common British artillery piece of the Great War. Twelve thousand of them were built and together they fired over 100 million rounds. With a range of 6,525 yards and operated by a crew of ten, the gun and limber were pulled by six horses. Now a very rare survivor and still fully functional, the gun was acquired by Sir Charles ffoulkes, then honorary curator and the first secretary of the Imperial War Museum, in 1921. It can now be seen at the Royal Armouries Museum of Artillery at Fort Nelson. The uniforms for the photo shoot were kindly provided by The Brockhurst Artillery, a group of Great War enthusiasts who regularly drill and perform the public firing of this gun at Fort Nelson, near Portsmouth. (Photograph courtesy of David Perkins)

Introduction

Like the ancient capital of Wessex, of which it forms a part, Salisbury Plain defies exact definition. I first became aware of the Plain through the pages of Thomas Hardy. As a young boy growing up in the enclosed suburban streets of London, it seemed to me, like Egdon Heath, a wilderness unwelcoming to the intrusion of man.

Stonehenge and the numerous archaeological remains in this area of South Wiltshire constantly remind us that people have lived in the region for many hundreds of years. Although seemingly bleak and unwelcoming, its rolling chalk downland has provided ideal grazing for multitudes of sheep. Gradually village communities developed along its valleys. Artists have found it an area of great beauty, and nature-lovers a haven where birds, beasts and flora have flourished – this despite the intervention of the army.

To many the army is both sinner and saint. We resent the faceless powers that deny us access, yet by restricting entry to large tracts of the Plain they hold back the forces of commercialism. They also protect the natural life – astonishing in the face of a century of military bombardment!

This book appears on the eve of a centenary. The year 1997 celebrates one hundred years of the army presence on the Plain. After the hard lessons of the Boer War there was a change in the tide of military affairs. Traditional, rather than formal, training had proved inadequate to prepare soldiers for mobility and good use of cover. Somewhere with a more open, more vast expanse of ground than Aldershot was needed. Somewhere close to London and the strategic port of Southampton.

Salisbury Plain provided a very acceptable solution. It was an ideal geographical position and had an open, grassy terrain suitable for large scale manoeuvres, for deploying infantry, cavalry and horse-drawn artillery. It also had the Avon for practising river crossings. What is more, with the severe agricultural depression effecting the price of land from the 1880s to the 1920s, there was no shortage of willing sellers.

In 1897 the army was able to gain a tentative foothold at Bulford, Market Lavington and – its greatest coup – the Tedworth Estate, where the first permanent barracks were built in 1903. As other segments of the Plain were purchased the nucleus of the camps we see today was formed. At the outbreak of war in 1914 a framework already existed to train the huge influx of men from the British Isles and every country of the Empire.

The middle section of this book attempts to show the human picture of those early years of military activity on the Plain. It is not a particularly pretty picture. Despite the camp comradeship (depicted by a myriad of commercial photographers of the time), there were floods to contend with, cold and mud, the increasing sickness endured by men under canvas with no means of drying wet clothes. Some might consider this the ideal preparation for the miseries of the Western Front! These images stand out vividly in my mind. Likewise the funerals of brave young airmen whose graves at Netheravon are stark reminders of the uncertainties of pioneer flying.

Civilian life in the villages continued the age-old preoccupation with the annual agricultural cycles. The section on Amesbury shows the development of Amesbury as a town. As the century progressed it became a centre of services and communications to the army as the railway and its commercial life grew. Like Salisbury, Warminster and other surrounding towns, its butchers, bakers, market gardeners and building contractors found this a period of expansion and prosperity.

Although we have concentrated on the early years of military involvement, the chapter on Imber reminds us that – apart from the enormous cost in service personnel – a social cost inevitably has to be paid in any war. Imber was probably the most remote settlement on Salisbury Plain, being seven miles from the nearest town, Warminster. Between 1928 and 1932 it was purchased by the War Office. At the end of 1943, so that the American Forces could train there, its 150 villagers were given six weeks notice of eviction. Despite promises at the time, the villagers have never been allowed to return. Today access remains restricted to certain days of the year. Each September a dwindling number of villagers continue to attend the annual memorial service in St Giles Church.

Our final section breaks away from the general theme. It presents an overview of the Plain through the camera of Austin Underwood, a professional photographer, journalist and teacher who lived in Amesbury and knew the area intimately. Austin was a radical thinker who translated his convictions into actions over a whole range of local and national issues. Of these his support for the Amesbury By-pass and the Association for the Restoration of Imber stand out like beacons. It would be impossible to reflect on all his work so we have hit upon one period only – the Sixties – when South East Wiltshire, the area portrayed in this book, was beginning to emerge from the shadow of world war and develop a new individuality.

Peter has spent much time in selecting the photographs we see here. They have come from numerous sources apart from his own vast library and reflect the generosity of many Plainsmen and women. I know he would want to acknowledge his debt to them and to those other travelling photographers like Tom Fuller of Amesbury and Albert Marett of Shrewton – both mentioned in this book – whose tireless efforts produced thousands of photographs depicting life on Salisbury Plain in all its facets.

Rex Sawyer
October 1996

One
Amesbury

FIRST WORLD WAR TROOPS MARCHING THROUGH THE TOWN. At the beginning of the twentieth century this thriving and historic community became the 'market town' for the army camps that were developing on Salisbury Plain. Countless officers stayed at the local inns and guest houses, including the George Hotel and the New Inn which can both be seen in this picture. The iron gates on the extreme left lead to the Methodist church built in 1900.

AMESBURY TOWN BRASS BAND IN AROUND 1890. Very little is known about the early history of the band as no clear records appear to have survived, but it has been discovered that two bands were in existence at one time in the nineteenth century. This is the earliest known photograph of the band which is believed to have developed from a fife and drum band formed in 1868. It was founded by bandmaster Edward G. Harrison.

TRAVELLERS AT AMESBURY AT AROUND THE TIME OF THE FIRST WORLD WAR. One can only estimate how many gypsies were living in South Wiltshire during the early twentieth century but one thing is clear: at times it was a very inhospitable place to live. This is a rare picture, taken before the restrictions of modern life intruded on their naturally nomadic existence. Basket and peg making, horse dealing and fortune telling are just a few of the more obvious ways in which they acquired money.

A LADY, A NURSE, A CHOW AND A NORWEGIAN HOUND. Lady Florence Caroline Mathilde Antrobus is pictured here with her friends in the grounds of Amesbury Abbey. She was the wife of Colonel Sir Edmund Antrobus. They had one son, also named Edmund, who was educated at Eton. Like his father, he was an officer in the Grenadier Guards but, sadly, he was killed in action in France in October 1914. The photograph was taken before 1912.

A MEETING OF THE HUNT IN THE GROUNDS OF AMESBURY ABBEY. These are thought to be the hounds and members of the Tedworth Hunt, who gathered here frequently during the early years of the twentieth century. The fashions worn by the individuals pictured here would suggest that this is a hunting scene from the 1930s. The Antrobus family purchased the Abbey in 1824. It was sold in 1979 and is now a nursing home.

THOMAS LIONEL FULLER, AMESBURY'S FIRST PROFESSIONAL PHOTOGRAPHER.
Born at Tonbridge, Kent, he came to Amesbury in 1911 and obtained a contract to produce photographs for the army. After serving with the Royal Flying Corps during the First World War, he returned to Amesbury and concentrated on his commercial photography business. The quality and range of his aviation, military and civilian photographs is probably unrivalled. Taken in August 1911, this photograph shows Tom 'Pop' Fuller outside his first photographic premises in Flower Lane. The wooden and corrugated tin shed was formerly used as a coffin manufactory by Bishops, builders and undertakers. Among the photographic paraphernalia that can be seen here is a brass and mahogany bellows camera and tripod, several beer bottles (probably containing chemicals) and boxes of 5 by 7in. glass photographic plates. There are also some leather camera cases, a black cloth (which covers the photographer's head), and, on the right, a mobile darkroom for developing plates in the field. Thankfully, many of Mr Fuller's photographs have survived and the business of T.L. Fuller continues to function in the capable hands of his son, who is popularly known as 'Jim'. He can be seen in the lower of the two photographs on the opposite page.

THE 1ST AMESBURY SCOUT TROOP IN AUGUST 1912. The Troop was formed in June 1910 with Mr D. Fairbrass the inaugural Scoutmaster. Primrose scarves were worn. The Troop had just returned from their annual summer camp when Mr E.J. Brown took this picture. He apologised to Scoutmaster Hillier (extreme left) for the slightly blurred appearance on his side of the photograph. This was due to poor light.

TOM FULLER'S SON, DAUGHTERS AND GRANDCHILD IN 1941. 'Pop' and Harriet Fuller had six children. Pictured from left to right are Winifred (Amesbury Police), Nancy (still at school), Jim (RAF), Ethel (WRENS), Helen (Short Brothers, aircraft manufaturers), Rosa (Land Army and later WRENS). Winifred's daughter, Valerie, can be seen in front. The photograph was taken in the garden of Fovant House, which is now the Fairlawn Hotel. The family moved into the converted stables which had been the weaving sheds of the Stonehenge Woollen Industry.

THE STAFF AT CHAPLIN AND COMPANY'S DEPOT IN SALISBURY STREET, 1919.
Charles Mundy stands second from the left in the front row and Percy Hunt is on the extreme
left at the back. Cecil Scott is second from the right in the middle row and below him, to the
right of the front row, is Mr Heather, who wears a bowler hat. Mr Yeates is seated on the left of
the middle row. Several horse-drawn wagons can be seen parked under the canopy in the
background. These were used for removal work, warehousing and parcel carrying. Pickfords
took over the site which was later cleared and re-developed. Chaplin's Place can be found here
today.

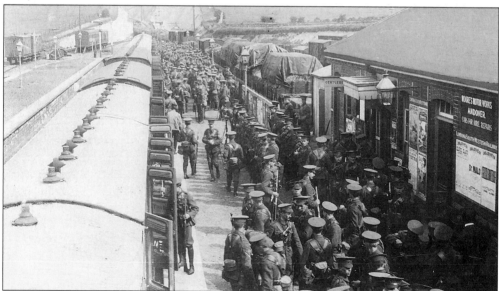

SOLDIERS DISEMBARKING AT AMESBURY STATION. These are the men of Princess
Beatrice's Own Isle of Wight Rifles who marched onward to their summer training ground at
Bustard Camp in July 1910. Amesbury railway station was opened in 1902 and with the
outbreak of war in 1914 a new line was constructed to serve the rapidly growing army camps in
the Larkhill area.

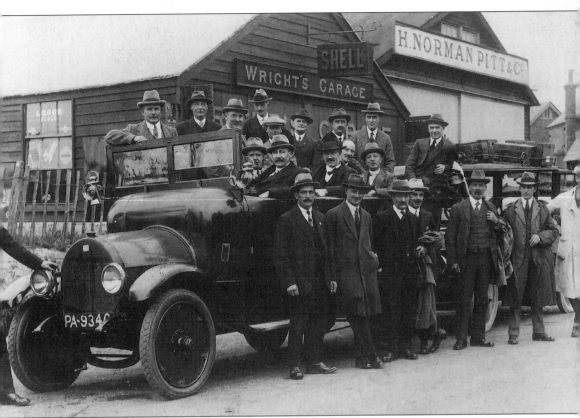

AN AMESBURY PARISH COUNCILLORS OUTING, 1923. Among those pictured in the back row are Major Martin, Mr Attwater, Harry James (Council Chairman), Thomas Matthews (general builder), William Hough (jeweller, watch and clock maker), William Witt (shopkeeper) and Frank Hale. In the second row we can see Mr Sloan (garage proprietor), Mr Robbins and Mr Marles sen. Among those standing beside the vehicles are Mac Wright (coach owner), George Scott, Mr Marles jun., Frank Tucker (shopkeeper), Sydney Hinxman (gardener) and Tom Wright, who is wearing a white driver's coat and a peaked cap. The leading vehicle is an ex-War Department Buick (PA9340) which in 1922 was fitted with a black 16-seat charabanc body by the Salisbury Carriage Works of Wilton Road, Salisbury. The day-trippers are assembled outside Wright's Garage and H. Norman Pitt's premises in Salisbury Street. Logan Homecare is the present occupier of the site.

PHILIP WESTON'S AND DICKY BIRD'S SHOPS IN FLOWER LANE. Dicky Bird was an official provider of accommodation to members of the Cyclists' Touring Club. He was a confectioner, a grocer, a tobacconist, and he served teas and refreshments. Mr Weston, pictured with his wife 'Auntie', ran a similar business here until around 1936. There are numerous signs on his shop highlighting some of the well-known products that could be bought there: Fry's Cocoa and Chocolate, Lyon's Tea, Orange Crush cordial (their motto was 'Every Day of the Year'), Mansion Polish and Glazier Mints.

Opposite: WILLIAM 'BUBBLO' WORSDELL AND HIS HANDSOME HACKNEY. Tom Fuller took this photograph of Mr Worsdell with his sparkling new taxi in the car park at the George Hotel in 1912 or 1913. The vehicle is a French-grey coloured 'Hotchkiss Torpedo' built by Hotchkiss et Cie of St Denis in France. It has a cape cart hood, Sankey wheels and carbide gas lamps. Bill was one of Amesbury's best known characters. He was born in Flower Lane and worked as a hackney carriage driver for more than fifty years. Having set up in business with one of the first mobile stores in the area, he travelled around the growing army camps with a horse and trolley, selling fruit and confectionery. He died in 1971 at the age of 80.

FRANK TUCKER'S TRAVELLER AT THE TIME OF THE FIRST WORLD WAR. Mr Tucker was a draper and outfitter. His shop was to be found in School Lane. He was also Chairman of Amesbury Parish Council. The role of his 'outrider' would be very similar to that of a modern day 'Sales Rep'. He would travel around the army camps on Salisbury Plain in his company vehicle, presenting quality goods to the officers and gentlemen. Product samples were carried in the boxes that can be seen on the back of the carriage.

AMESBURY HIGH STREET IN THE EARLY TWENTIES. Bertram and Barbara Hale's shops can be seen on the left of the picture. One could say that there were several sides to their business! In the window nearest to the camera, under the 'Draper and Outfitter' sign, numerous hats are displayed with prices starting at 5s 6d. There are also some shirts, handkerchiefs and ties on show. In the right window, under the 'Boots and Shoes' lettering, one can see a selection of shirt collars, gentlemen's striped undergarments and footwear. Next door is the post office, where Mrs Hale was the registered sub-postmistress; a window poster advertises the following products and services: 'Stationery and Fancy Goods, Monthly Magazines, Novels and Fashion Books, Local and Other Postcards, Sole Agent for 'Goss' China'. In the distance the George Hotel comes into view. This building is thought to have been built originally as a pilgrims' hostel, annexed to Amesbury Abbey. More recently, it has been a coaching inn visited by Edward VII, then Prince of Wales. When this photograph was taken the hotel had just been enlarged and renovated. Modern sanitation and electric lighting were installed in every room and a telephone line was connected. Telephone number 8 was allocated. Thomas Sparrow was the manager at that time.

Opposite: WITT'S, CONFECTIONERS, STATIONERS AND FANCY GOODS DEALER. William Witt started out in business before the First World War, being proprietor of a hairdressing salon in the High Street. By the mid-1920s he had opened this shop in Church Street. The photograph appears to have been taken at Easter as there are a number of chocolate eggs on display in the left window. There are two 'Penny Sweet Machines' fixed to the wall on the right of the shop entrance; these dispense Fruit Pastels and Sharps Toffees. In the right-hand window a range of Fuller's postcards can be seen.

18

THE FIRST AMESBURY CO-OPERATIVE STORE. This branch, the first of three, was opened in 1912. The manager was Joe Robbins, a Warminster resident who came to live at The Pound in Salisbury Road, Amesbury. For many years he served as a parish councillor, as did his son, John, who died recently. There is a wide selection of Co-op own brand products on show in the window, including sugar, Chick Feed, tea, coffee and cocoa. There is a stack of enamel saucepans displayed in the doorway ranging in price from 4s 3d for the large pan at the bottom to 1s for the smaller items on top. The blackboard advertises 'Prime English Cheese at 9d per lb. Try our Bread and Cakes. You Cannot Beat Them.'

A SNOWY MORNING IN APRIL 1917. Taken on the third day of the month, the photograph shows the junction of London Road and High Street, with Countess Road leading off to the left. The building on the right is the YMCA. The large sign that stands in the middle of the picture informs the reader that 'This Freehold Building Land For Sale in Lots of 25 Ft and Upwards. Apply Wort and Way, Castle Street, Salisbury.' Countess Court occupies the site today.

QUEENSBERRY BRIDGE. First World War soldiers are watering their horses. The bridge was built by the 3rd Duke of Queensberry in 1775 at his own expense. It formed part of a new road from the west that was developed by the Amesbury Turnpike Trust. In 1957 a single-span steel bridge was erected alongside the original to make it safer for pedestrians to cross the river.

Two
Imber

MONKEY STREET AT THE DAWN OF A NEW CENTURY. Many Imber cottages were thatched. They had whitewashed walls and well-tended gardens. The cottages shown nearest to the camera were occupied by the Pearce family, Thomas and Ann Potter, Jemima Meaden and Betsy Meaden (no relation). The thatched house beyond was the home of the Tinnam family. The Bell Inn comes into view in the distance. Dating from 1769, only the shell remains today.

WILLIAM ROBERT DEAN OF EAST FARM (1839-1905). William married Harriet Hooper and fathered the children seen on the opposite page. He was the grandson of Matthew Dean, who was robbed by four highwaymen when returning from Devizes Market in 1839. With the aid of three others, Matthew pursued the robbers for three hours across Chitterne Down until one of them collapsed and died of exhaustion and the others were captured. This story is told on the Robbers' Stone which can still be seen near Gore Cross.

IMBER HIGH STREET IN THE EARLY TWENTIETH CENTURY. A well can be seen outside John Cruse's cottage. On one particular occasion, after an argument, he swept up all the china and silver from the table and threw them down the well, from whence they were never retrieved. One can also just see the post box that was set into the wall of his cottage. Apart from the post office, this was the only mail collection point in the village. Following the path of the stream known as Imber Dock, which dried up during the summer months, our eyes are lead to Tinker's Barn.

THE BROTHERS DEAN. A well-known Wiltshire farming family since the early years of the nineteenth century, the Deans managed three out of the five farms at Imber. They provided one churchwarden and sometimes both in almost unbroken succession from 1791 until the eviction in 1943 – a long record of village service for one family. Our picture depicts four of the five children of William and Harriet Dean: Willie (born 1872), Fred (born 1875), Frank (born 1874) and Ted (born 1877). Sidney was born in 1884, after this photograph was taken.

GRANNY STAPLES' SHOP IN AROUND 1912. Church Lane met the High Street in an area known as the Barracks. This was a jumble of cottages – in many ways the hub of the village. Ann Staples' grocery and provisions shop was to be found there. Probably the oldest house in the village when this photograph was taken, it was sadly destroyed by fire at around the time of the First World War. Here also was the smithy of James Staples, Ann's husband, until his death in 1888.

SEAGRAM'S FARM, ALSO KNOWN AS EAST FARM, IN THE THIRTIES. Edward Seagram owned the farm a hundred years before this photograph was taken, and records show that Matthew Dean was the occupier in 1838. His family had lived here for several generations. During floods, the water entered the house right up to the withdrawing room fireplace.

IMBER POST OFFICE AFTER THE FIRST WORLD WAR. Before 1914 there was no post office in the village and letters arrived by foot messenger from Codford St Mary at about 9a.m. The only post box was situated at John Cruse's cottage. It was cleared daily at 4.20p.m. John Carter was the sub-postmaster throughout the 1920s and 1930s and he can just be seen here outside the post office. A carpenter by profession, he was the first person in the village to own a telephone – his number was 'Imber 1'.

JAMES AND ELIZA DANIELS OUTSIDE THEIR COTTAGE. They lived here at number 7 High Street for many years. Eliza came from the Mundy family, of Tilshead. James was an agricultural labourer. He died in 1920 and was the last person to be buried in the Baptist Chapel graveyard at Imber.

STEAM THRESHING AT TINKER'S FARM IN THE TWENTIES. Billie Burgess stands nearest to the camera, then Sidney Dean, William Pearce, John Marsh and Silas Pearce, who was the father of Emily Daniels. Harry Marsh and his son can be seen on top of the threshing machine. The steam traction engine is believed to be a single-cylinder 8 nhp model (No. 7269) that was made by Wallis and Steevens of Basingstoke in 1912. It was supplied to Frederick James Dean of Tinker's Farm on 7 June that year. Now owned by an enthusiast in Essex, at one time it was named 'The Panther'. Having been re-registered it now carries the number PU 3378. Another engine that is known to have worked in the village was also made by Wallis and Steevens. A 6 nhp model (No. 7001), it was delivered to Dean Brothers of Imber on 23 August 1907. It's Wiltshire registration number was HR3537.

HENRY CRUSE, THE LAST OF THE PEELERS. Born in Imber in 1840, he enrolled as a police officer at the age of 26 and served with the Wiltshire Constabulary for thirty years. During that time he was stationed at Bradford-on-Avon, Broadchalke, Corsham, Marlborough, Melksham, Mere, New Swindon, Old Swindon and Yarnbrook. He died in 1935. His grandson joined the force in the same year and retired with the rank of sergeant in 1965.

ALBERT NASH, THE IMBER BLACKSMITH. After his death in 1888, James Staples was succeeded by William Nash and then by his son, Albert, who is believed to have died of a broken heart soon after the evacuation in December 1943. He is pictured here at the smithy in around 1920 with Janet, a horse that was owned by Lieutenant (later Captain) Arthur Cecil Williams and his wife Hilda (née Hooper) of Brown's Farm. Hilda was from another of the old Imber farming families.

A REVIVALIST MEETING BEFORE THE FIRST WORLD WAR. This grassed area of the village was known as the Barley Ground and many events have been held here. It could be said that this was the community sports and recreation ground. On this particular occasion, Mr and Mrs Ware came to preach the gospel, and they stayed for about a fortnight. The vicar of Imber, Revd Charles Watling, announced his displeasure from the pulpit because his flock went straight to the meeting tent after leaving church. A number of shepherds and dogs can be seen in the field, having just returned from their day's work. Imber Court comes into view in the distance.

Opposite: THE BAPTIST CHAPEL AT THE TIME OF THE FIRST WORLD WAR. On the Warminster side of the Bell Inn, a track led up to the chapel and a small burial ground which stood well back from the High Street. The chapel, seating 180, was built in 1839. Founder members were Thomas Found, James Pearce, Isaac Carter and William Grant. There are still a few gravestones to be seen in the burial ground: the earliest legible inscription is that of 'Fanny, wife of Charles Ashley', who died in 1875. The most recent stone appears to be that of James Daniels, who passed away in 1920.

JOHN CRUSE, A DEW POND MAKER
(1811-1882). Of the many trades practised at
Imber, dew pond making was the best known.
It was an hereditary craft, practised by several
families over many generations. John Cruse
was later joined by his son Joel, and together
they built mud walls and laid floors in many
of the cottages. The last surviving dew pond
maker was Charles White, who died in 1927.

THE LADIES' CORONATION COMMITTEE, 1911. Pictured from left to right in the front row are Fanny Matthew's (née Carter), Mrs Bundy, Mrs Tinnans (who ran a shop in the village for a short time) and Ada Cruse (who brought up her niece, Phyllis Wright). Ada was very lady-like. She liked to be called 'Miss' Cruse. In the back row we can see Annie Pearce (later Mrs Nash, whose wedding photograph is reproduced on page 32), Julie Pearce (her father was one of Mr Hooper's shepherds) and Eliza Tinnam (later Mrs Coleman).

Opposite: IMBER IN FLOOD, JANUARY 1911. Flooding was a constant concern in the past. In 1757, flood water came from the direction of Broken Cross, Ladywell and Southdown House. The walls of the mud-built cottages were undermined and several buildings collapsed. It is believed there was also some loss of life. Here, we are looking towards East Farm, which can be seen in the distance, with the buildings of Brown's Farm coming into view on the right. At the time of the evacuation in 1943, the houses on the left were occupied by Enos and Fanny Matthews and the Marsh family.

WHIT MONDAY AT IMBER. The feast day of the Imber Slate Club, when the procession, usually led by the Lavington Band, would march to the big barn on Imber Court Farm for their lunch. The children, who are obviously enjoying themselves, can be seen here outside the school. The boys are carrying red and white spotted handkerchiefs containing a plate, a knife and a fork for their lunch. On one occasion a local farmer named Willie Hooper was asked to give the vote of thanks. A shy man, he said, 'Well, I enjoyed my dinner, I hope you did!' and sat down.

THE WEDDING OF ANNIE PEARCE AND DAN NASH. Dating from the First World War period, the photograph was taken outside a cottage that could be found opposite Tinker's Farm. Nelson Carter and his sister Fanny can be seen on the left in the back row, then comes Walter Coleman, Dan Nash (brother of Albert), Annie Pearce and her brother Harry, then Kate Wyatt (half-sister of the bride). The name of the man on the extreme right is not recorded. Seated left to right are Mary Goddard (later Mrs Ketteringham), Ella Meaden (daughter of Jemima and Silas Meaden, who was a shepherd), Percy Wyatt (son of Kate and Arthur), Lizzie Goddard (sister of May), Sidney Pearce (with beard) and, on his lap, John Wyatt (son of Kate).

Opposite: CHRISTINE GORDON JONES WITH HER BROTHER TREVOR, JULY 1927. They were the children of Ernest Imrie Jones, vicar of Imber, and his wife Hilda. Also shown is their pet dog 'Cuppy' and the children's cart named 'Jamie Chubb'. The children are in the paddock in front of Imber Vicarage. Christine recalls that they had very few toys. 'The cart was fun, however, you could sit in it and steer it.'

A RUDGE MOTORCYCLE IN THE YARD AT BROWN'S FARM. Mollie Dean (now Mrs Archer-Smith) is at the front and Gladwyn Williams is at the back. Gladwyn was the daughter of Captain Arthur Cecil Williams, of Brown's Farm, and his first wife, who had died. The motorcycle is driven by Glyn Williams (Gladwyn's cousin) but they are not going far because it has been left resting on its stand.

THE VICAR OF IMBER AND HIS WIFE.
Ernest Imrie Jones was vicar of Imber from
1925 to 1928. The couple were
photographed in the back garden of the
Vicarage, with the vegetable garden, coach
house and stables in the background. The
family left Imber in 1928 and moved to the
Vicarage at Alvediston.

THE INTERIOR OF ST GILES CHURCH
BEFORE THE EVACUATION. Although
the church is now empty, some of its former
treasures are housed in other nearby
churches to which they were removed. The
fine Norman font can now be seen at
Brixton Deverill and the bells are at
Edington. An account survives of a fight
which took place at St Giles in 1646
between two local girls. Their complaints
were later heard before a magistrate but the
result is not recorded.

A VIEW OF THE VICARAGE FROM THE TOWER OF ST GILES CHURCH. The vicarage was an imposing four square building with stone mullioned windows and pinnacles. It was demolished in 1969 having been severely damaged by the army. Sadly, all that remains now is the well which has been completely filled with rubble. The large white building just seen in the distance is the Baptist Chapel.

ST GILES, THE PARISH CHURCH OF IMBER. Dating from the thirteenth and fourteenth centuries, the church is believed to have been built on the site of an earlier Norman church. Buried in the adjacent churchyard are the remains of many former village inhabitants. There is also the grave of a man named Grimes. He was one of two brigands who were shot dead on Saturday 2 June 1716 having robbed several persons returning from Warminster Market.

THE IMBER CHOIR AND BELLRINGERS' OUTING IN 1929. Pictured from left to right are Bernie Wright, Albert Daniels (shepherd to the Deans), Harry Marsh, Stuart Carter, John Carter, Jimmy Nash, Revd William Walser (seated, the last vicar of Imber), Tom Danniell, William Meaden, Dennis Wyatt, Harwood Daniels, Ellis Daniels, Percy Daniels and Frank Carpenter, who was nicknamed 'Tredoodle'. The charabanc (MR 9319) is a light-blue-coloured Reo (R.E. Olds) that was operated by Alfred Jefferies (also a glove manufacturer) of Station Road, Warminster. It can be seen here at The Canal (now New Canal) in Salisbury.

'FOREVER IMBER.' Many people felt that Imber should have been returned to the villagers after the Second World War. Following the end of the Defence of the Realm Act in 1960, Austin Underwood, an Amesbury Councillor, wrote to the newspapers saying that he was going to Imber and would like others to join him. On 22 January 1961 approximately 700 cars and 2,000 people travelled the muddy lanes and paths from Gore Cross to Imber. They were led by a tractor driven by Richard Hooper, the son of local farmers, Norris and Betty Hooper. This was the beginning of the 'Imber Shall Live' campaign, which sought to keep open for public use the rights of way and to re-establish Imber as a parish. The crusade continued throughout the 1960s.

Opposite: THE LAST HOUSES TO BE BUILT AT IMBER, 1935-37. They were built by several contractors, including Plumber and Hockey of Radstock and W.J. Morgan of Midsomer Norton. The project was part of a War Department scheme to modernise the village. It involved the construction of several blocks of 'new' homes and the demolition of more than thirty old cottages. Mrs Ada Cruse is believed to have been the occupier of the house shown on the left of the picture.

THE ANNUAL MEMORIAL SERVICE AT ST GILES CHURCH, 1967. Since 1961 a service has been held here on the first Saturday in September (the nearest to St Giles Day). It is the ideal opportunity for the dwindling numbers of former Imber friends and neighbours to meet and talk over old times. Miss Glanfield is seated next to the aisle on the left of the picture. Her brother Edgar was the vicar of Imber from 1917 to 1923. At the annual service she demanded – and received – transport from the army.

CANON RALPH DUDLEY AT THE ANNUAL REUNION SERVICE, 1969. Canon Dudley was the vicar of Edington with Imber, and he can be seen here talking to Gladys Mitchell, daughter of the last Imber blacksmith, Albert Nash. Mrs Davis of Gore Cross stands in the right foreground.

A CONFRONTATION AT GORE CROSS. In March 1961 the army went to the High Court and writs were served on the organisers of the 'Imber Shall Live' campaign to prevent the proposed public invasion of the village. At each assembly point, including the one shown here at Gore Cross, marshals were on duty to turn people back. The army were out in force also. Here can be seen a helicopter and a Saracen Armoured Personnel Carrier.

THE SAD REMAINS OF IMBER COURT. The Wadman family built Imber Court on the site of an earlier manor in the eighteenth century. They were the Lords of the Manor throughout the seventeen and eighteen hundreds and there were several memorials to them in the church. Later it was the home of the Dean family. A fine avenue of trees led from the house to the 'dog kennel', where a pack of hounds was kept. The house was burnt down in the 1920s but was soon restored by Holloways, builders, of London.

JUST LIKE OLD TIMES! A gathering outside the church after the reunion service at Imber in September 1969. Sydney Dean (last of the churchwardens before the village was evacuated) can be seen on the extreme left. Next to him is Enos Matthews, then Mrs Fanny Matthews, Mrs Nellie Rea, Percy E. Plank, Walter H. Coleman, Walter Plank, Mrs Ellen M. Coleman, Mrs Mollie Archer-Smith, Fred White, Mrs Dolly White and finally Fred Pearce.

Three

Around Ludgershall and Tidworth

A MINIATURE WAR. In the early 1930s a tank exercise was held on Salisbury Plain. Here we can see two Medium Mark II tanks of the 5th Battalion Royal Tank Corps (T132 and T142) climbing the hill out of Collingbourne Ducis. A number of spectators can be see at the bottom of the hill. The officers' cars are parked on the road adjacent to the Elementary School (built 1855) and the Church of St Andrew is also in view.

AN OFFICER TRAINING CORPS UNIT AT TIDWORTH PENNINGS IN 1913. Pictured here in various stages of readiness are the pupils of Blundells School. Some of them appear to be fully clothed while others are still eating their breakfasts. Each bell tent would seem to have accommodated six men in relative luxury. They are not sleeping on grass, as one would have imagined, but on raised wooden floors. There are approximately forty-five tents. Tidworth Park and Tidworth Pennings were usually allocated to units of the Officer Training Corps during the month of August. By 1914 Tidworth was the largest base on Salisbury Plain.

Opposite: A TRAINEE OFFICERS BOXING CONTEST AT TIDWORTH. An Officers Training Corps camp would include representatives from a number of public schools. The pupils would have been required to take part in a range of physical activities including boxing. The rules for this sport were laid down by the Army Boxing Association. This particular contest appears to have created a great deal of interest. The photograph was taken in the 1920s.

A VERY SMART TURNOUT AT TIDWORTH IN 1911. These young men attended a ten day Officer Training Corps camp at Tidworth Pennings at the beginning of August. They are pictured here during an inspection. A proficiency badge can be seen on the right arm of the soldier who stands nearest to the officer on the left of the group. High standards were always expected. A pencilled note has been written on the back of the original photograph: 'Our tent won the prize for the best kept one!'

A WOLSELEY-SIDDELEY OFFICERS CAR AT WINDMILL HILL CAMP, 1909. This is believed to be a Hampshire Yeomanry camp. 7-QMS Reg Toomer can be seen in the driving seat with Trooper Samways sitting beside him. Toomer has an inverted horseshoe on his right sleeve which would suggest he is a farrier. The elegant side-entry motor car carries the Hampshire registration number: AA2609. It has detachable wooden-rimmed wheels, white tyres, brass lamps and a folding hood. The seats are probably leather.

A GUN CARRIAGE AT WINDMILL HILL CAMP, 1905. These are the men of the 1st Hampshire Rifle Voluntary Corps. Such units were the forerunners of the Territorials formed three years later. This was the old method of transporting maxim guns on horse-drawn carriages. Later they were carried by truck.

THE HAMPSHIRE'S COOKHOUSE. The 7th Battalion Hampshire Regiment was encamped at Windmill Hill in 1909. Here we can see the regimental cooks turning out containers of food from the ovens that are just in view in the left foreground. An oven was constructed from a curved piece of corrugated iron covered with a thick layer of mud. A chimney pipe protruded from one end.

MEN OF THE ARMY SERVICE CORPS AT WINDMILL HILL CAMP, MAY 1915. There is
an air of informality in this photograph of a group of NCOs at Windmill Hill. The lieutenant in
the centre of the group holds a cigarette in his left hand, and the sergeant seated in the right
foreground is smoking a pipe. The Army Service Corps provided and maintained the life blood
of the British Army – its transport. One of the lads pictured here is named Bert. He sent this
postcard to Mr E. Burtenshaw of 28 Hampden Road, Brighton, with the following few words: 'I
am sending this photo of some of the chaps here, some don't look happy, but I believe theyre
alright (sic).'

THE KING AT LUDGERSHALL AT THE TIME OF THE FIRST WORLD WAR. The branch line from Ludgershall to Tidworth was frequently used to transport visiting VIPs. On 8 November 1917 King George V travelled to Ludgershall in the Royal Train. He then rode on a charger to Perham Down where he carried out an inspection of the troops. This picture was almost certainly taken on that occasion. We can see here numerous armed soldiers, seven or eight civilian police officers and a few smartly dressed gentlemen, one of whom was probably the Stationmaster, George H. Humphries.

Opposite: THE MANCHESTERS DETRAIN AT LUDGERSHALL, JULY 1906. Having arrived safely at Ludgershall railway station, these men from the 4th Voluntary Battalion Manchester Regiment are preparing to march to Windmill Hill Camp. The Ludgershall to Tidworth line was opened in 1901. It was the first railway to be built on the Plain with the primary objective of servicing the rapidly growing military camps. The trains were used to transport both men and their equipment. By 1907 it was noted that the quiet village of Ludgershall had become the busy entrepôt for the military centres of Salisbury Plain.

FIELD OVENS OF WHICH TO BE PROUD, AT PERHAM DOWN CAMP, 1912. These are the cooks of the 3rd Battalion Hampshire Regiment. Their ovens are much more elaborate than those depicted on page 45. The men are no doubt preparing themselves for a field inspection – even the utensils pictured on the left have been whitewashed! The sergeant standing in the foreground looks particularly pleased with himself: perhaps he feels the competition has already been won.

LONDON INFANTRY BRIGADE ON CHURCH PARADE AT PERHAM DOWN, 1913. These are the men of the 2nd Battalion. On 11 August one of them sent this postcard to Miss Elizabeth Mark, of 'Welbury', Rowsley Avenue, Hendon. 'Dear Lizzie, This is a rather good photo of the Church Parade last Sunday, although the battalion on the right of the square is not included. The 'LR' Base [Leisure and Recreation Base, perhaps?] is on the left in front of the YMCA Marquee. You won't be able to find me because I was right in the rear, being one of the collectors. Lancers are in barracks again at Tidworth and it is grand to see them out with their horses.' It is signed 'Bri'.

MEDIUM MARK II TANKS OF THE 6TH BATTALION, ROYAL TANK CORPS. The tank army is seen here moving forward to attack during a mechanised troops exercise near Perham Down in the late 1920s or early 1930s. A solitary motorcycle observer can also be seen. The group of spectators in the foreground would include some officers, their wives, local farmers and other guests.

WINSTON CHURCHILL INSPECTING MECHANISED FORCES AT PERHAM DOWN.
Mr Churchill, then Chancellor of the Exchequer, is pictured here with Colonel Commandant
Collins (left) and Lieutenant Colonel C.A. Bolton CBE (right). They are inspecting an
experimental gas-powered tank during Mr Churchill's visit to Salisbury Plain in September
1927. This was possibly the first exercise involving the 5th Battalion Royal Tank Corps as a
complete unit. On this occasion they were testing this special tank to see if it would run
satisfactorily on coal gas instead of petrol.

Opposite: A 'DRAGON' TAKING A SHORT-CUT THROUGH A CORNFIELD IN 1928.
The vehicle is a 30 cwt Crossley semi-tracked Field Artillery Tractor. The half-track con-
version was based on the French-built Kegresse rear bogies which incorporated continuous
rubber band tracks. It can be seen here near Perham Down, towing an 18-pounder field gun and
limber. It carries a gun crew of eight from the 9th Field Brigade, Royal Artillery.

A MARK VI LIGHT TANK OF THE 5TH BATTALION, ROYAL TANK CORPS. This three-man light tank was often used for reconnaissance purposes. It was introduced in the mid-1930s. The officer depicted here at Perham Down is unlikely to have been serving with the Royal Tank Corps at the time because he is not wearing a black beret. The Middlesex registration number, CMM 915, was issued in July 1952. It comes from a special series reserved for Government Departments.

THE GUARD ROOM AT LUCKNOW BARRACKS, TIDWORTH, IN AROUND 1910.
The Tedworth Estate was previously the home of Thomas Assheton Smith, a legendary master
of foxhounds. When the army began to acquire land on the Plain in 1897, the estate became its
most notable purchase. In 1904-05 eight permanent barracks were built along the valley. These
are still used in modified form today. All were named after celebrated Indian campaigns. Four of
them were to accommodate Infantry battalions: Aliwal, Assaye, Candahar and Mooltan. The
remaining four were set aside for Cavalry units: Bhurtpore, Delhi, Jellalabad and Lucknow.

Opposite: A YORKSHIRE LIGHT INFANTRY DISPLAY AT THE TIDWORTH TATTOO.
These are the men of the 1st Battalion King's Own Yorkshire Light Infantry. Military tattoos
were held at Tidworth from 1920 to 1935, enabling the public to see a different side of military
life. The entertainment would have included precision marching, massed bands, horse shows,
gymkhanas, physical training displays and free-fall parachuting. Although it was revived from
1966 to 1976 it was never repeated on the same scale.

'WASHING HIS SINS OUT.' These lads from the 1st Wiltshire Corps of Drums are having a bit of fun at Tidworth Barracks. The soldier in the tin bath is having his sins washed out. His colleagues appear to be scrubbing him with mops and a yard brush. The postcard picture was taken by W.H. Jones, photographer, of Ludgershall, and although it was produced in 1912 it was not sent through the post until thirty years later. It carries a London postmark of 1 October 1942.

THE FOOD PREPARATION AND DISTRIBUTION DEPOT AT TIDWORTH. The complex was to be found in Kirkee Road along the route of the Tidworth Military Railway. Stores were transported to the camp by a pair of tank engines named 'Betty' and 'Molly'. The horse-drawn vans pictured here were specifically designed for the transportation of food to the outlying camps on Salisbury Plain. The drivers were members of the Army Service Corps. The bakery and butchery sections shown here at the time of the First World War have since been demolished. There were also several warehouses and a flour store on the site.

THE INSIGNIA OF THE 9TH LANCERS. This unusual lance display with crown, cipher and gong is know by the regiment as either 'The Gong' or 'The Memorial'. It can be seen here at A Squadron, 9th Queen's Royal Lancers, at Moolton Barracks, Tidworth in April 1915. The display has travelled with the regiment wherever it has been stationed, and there is a photograph from 1930 which shows it at Sialkot in India. It was amalgamated with the memorial of the 12th Lancers in 1960, when the two regiments combined.

THE ROYAL SCOTS GREYS REGIMENT AT TIDWORTH, 1909. Before the First World War army life on Salisbury Plain was heavily dependent on the horse. Mules and horses were to be found everywhere and in every field of military activity. In this photograph we see some very classy representatives in the horse lines of the Royal Scots Greys. The Married Quarters and the Sergeants' Mess can be seen in the background.

THE REFRESHMENT COUNTER AT TIDWORTH SOLDIERS HOME, 1908. There are no obvious clues to be found on this photograph to suggest which particular establishment is shown here. The original item comes from a small collection of postcards and photographs assembled by Sister Dora Stephenson, who was associated with the Ian Hamilton Soldiers Home at Tidworth. We leave you to come to your own conclusions. (A photograph of the Ian Hamilton Soldiers Home has been reproduced on the opposite page.) The shiny new urn in the centre of this picture dispenses tea and coffee. The shelves are full of many good things, including bottles of Grape Wine and Fruit Cordial. There are boxes of Fry's Sweet Chocolate and Fry's Chocolate Creams, containers of pocket pencils and boxes of matches, and a selection of Salisbury view postcards from the 'Peacock' series. There is a leg of Harris's Wiltshire Bacon (from Calne) and a box of tobacco products from H. Stevens and Company of Silver Street, Salisbury. There are also packets of headache powders, 'Rose Tooth Powders' and Sedlitz Powders –whatever they are!

THE IAN HAMILTON WESLEYAN SOLDIERS HOME, TIDWORTH. Opened on 4 July 1908, this was the first centre to provide for the welfare of the many soldiers stationed in the new barracks at Tidworth. The building included facilities for concerts, games, study and refreshments. It was named after Lieutenant General Sir Ian Hamilton, Commander-in-Chief at the time. The building can still be seen opposite the Tidworth Oval, near the main entrance to the barracks.

THE CHURCH OF ENGLAND SOLDIERS INSTITUTE AT TIDWORTH. In 1908 plans were drawn up for a Church of England Institute for soldiers. This centre was opened by General Sir Charles Douglas and the Bishop of Salisbury in August 1910. It adjoined the Electric Cinema (often called the Institute Cinema) and was demolished in 1965. The track of the Tidworth Military Railway can be seen in the foreground.

CLARENDON TERRACE, TIDWORTH IN THE TWENTIES. The row of houses pictured to the left can still be found in Grand Trunk Road but they are now unoccupied. At the time of the photograph they were the warrant officers married quarters. William Osmond, a pastry cook and confectioner of 13 Fisherton Street, Salisbury, appears to be making a delivery with his horse and cart.

A ROYAL FIELD ARTILLERY CAMP AT TIDWORTH PARK. The horse lines are shown to the left of the photograph and the gun park is to the right. The soldiers were accommodated in the neat rows of bell tents that can also be seen on the right. The bigger tents were reserved for communal activities such as eating, reading and writing, etc. The two large marquees were provided by Simonds, the brewers and caterers. These were very popular places, known as 'wet canteens'. The camp kitchen would have been positioned out of view to the left of the area shown in the picture.

Opposite: THE TIDWORTH GARRISON THEATRE BEFORE THE FIRST WORLD WAR. With the need to provide entertainment for thousands of troops, the Garrison Theatre was opened in 1909. The first event to be staged there was a boxing competition organised by the Royal Fusiliers. The hall has had a long and varied history, and among those who have performed are Dame Nellie Melba, Will Hay, Bob Hope, James Cagney, Henry Cooper and Frankie Vaughan. The first manager was Bert Pickernell, who was succeeded by his son Ken in 1947 and his grandson Tony (the present manager) in 1987 – almost a century of service from one family. The theatre stands at the junction of Bazaar Road and Lowa Road.

COFFEE BAR STAFF AT PARKHOUSE photographed before 1920 at a Royal Marine Light Infantry camp (RMLI) at Parkhouse. The camp ground was situated north of the Amesbury to Andover Road (A303). It was one of six original camps that were created at Tidworth during the early years of the Twentieth Century. The RMLI, together with the Royal Marine Artillery, were formed during the First World War.

THE SERGEANTS MESS STAFF AND 'TWIG' AT PARKHOUSE CAMP, AUGUST 1913. This photographic postcard appears to have been sent to George's sweetheart, Miss A. Hart of 48 Milkwood Road, Herne Hill, London. 'Dear A, This is a snapshot of my cooks and waiters and Twig the cat. Just ready for tea. Fondest love, George.'

Four

Around Bulford, Durrington, Netheravon and Upavon

BULFORD CAMP INSTITUTE BAZAAR. Held at the Market House in Salisbury (now the Public Library) in May 1901, the event was organised to help raise funds for the building of a new Church of England Soldiers Institute at Bulford Camp. Among the numerous local and national VIPs who attended the bazaar are the individuals seated at the front of this group. Pictured from left to right are the Duchess of Somerset, Mrs Wordsworth, Sir Redvers Buller, the Bishop of Salisbury (John Wordsworth), Lady Audrey Buller and the Mayor of Salisbury, Councillor Mr Henry George Gregory. General Buller was a member of the influential War Office Salisbury Plain Committee which was created in 1897.

HOME SWEET HOME! Someone has thoughtfully scribbled a note on the back of the original photograph: 'Rick at the door of his hut at Bulford Camp, May 22nd 1911'. It is a pity that the author did not indicate which one of these characters is Rick. We are also unaware of which hut he occupied – was it Rose Villa or number 65? One thing is fairly clear, however: they are erecting new wooden army huts at the camp, huts designed to accommodate 10 to 12 men. They were heated by a single stove. The builders' huts were easily moved from one site to another. Running on large cast iron wheels, they could be pulled along by a traction engine, a tractor or a pair of cart horses. They were constructed of timber and corrugated iron, and are similar to those used by shepherds and road builders. The accommodation was surprisingly comfortable, incorporating a stove, a cupboard and at least one bed.

MISS PERK'S SOLDIERS' HOME AT BULFORD CAMP, 1912. Opened in 1902, the home occupied the present site of the Bulford Garrison Roman Catholic church. A Salisbury Plain guide book of around 1905 describes the institute as 'a handsome and commodious building, pleasantly situated, and containing excellent restaurant, devotional rooms, bedrooms and bath rooms. All completely fitted up and furnished in a comfortable manner.' In this photograph we can see some soldiers relaxing in the Reading Room.

Opposite: THE CHURCH OF ENGLAND SOLDIERS' INSTITUTE, 1905. Built in Plumer Road, Bulford, at a cost of nearly £7,000, the new soldiers' home was opened by Lieutenant Colonel Stirling in June 1903. Charles Thomas Powell was the first manager. The entrance door that can be seen under the canopy to the right of the building leads to 'the Refreshment Room'. The hall on the left was set aside for Reading, Writing and Games. Although still in use during the Second World War, the facility was later demolished.

THE KIWI AT SLING PLANTATION. The image was constructed by New Zealanders at the time of the First World War. It was cut into Beacon Hill by soldiers waiting to return home. Precise dimensions of the flightless bird were supplied by a specialist from the Natural History Museum in London. These were scaled up to create a Kiwi measuring 420 ft in length. The beak is 50 ft long.

NEW ZEALAND BRIGADE ORCHESTRA AT SLING IN AROUND 1914. The musicians are from the New Zealand 4th Reserves at Sling Plantation. There are eleven wind instrumentalists represented here, plus eight who play stringed instruments. The conductor and percussionists bring the total number of performers to twenty-two. Sling Plantation Camp has been described as 'unloved, bleak and lonely', but it did have relatively comfortable huts and a good range of social activities.

SLING PLANTATION CAMPS AT THE BEGINNING OF THE FIRST WORLD WAR.
Following the outbreak of hostilities, the War Department hoped to accommodate all troops in
huts by November 1914. The appalling weather that prevailed at that time, however, prevented
the civilian contractors from achieving that goal. In October approximately 900 Canadians had
arrived on the Plain. They were almost immediately set to work building huts to replace tents
like those shown here. Despite their tremendous efforts large numbers of men were still sleeping
under canvas by Christmas. In this photograph we can see a line of general service wagons in
the foreground, with the camp kitchen and two canteen tents just right of centre. There are
horse lines and bell tents to the left with large stacks of hay or straw in the middle ground. The
Red Cross tents on the extreme right are more spaced out to help prevent the spread of
infection. A second camp, set out in much the same way as the first, dominates the background.

BULFORD CAMP FIRE STATION IN THE THIRTIES. This building was found near the junction of Rawlinson Road and Signal Street. It was still in use in 1985. The fire engine on the left is a Thornycroft six-wheeler with a Braidwood body (developed by James Braidwood, later Chief Officer of the London Fire Engine Establishment). The crew would be seated back to back along the sides of the machine. It carried an extension ladder and a first-aid hose reel which is mounted amidships. The second appliance is a four-wheeled Dennis, which is built to a very similar design. Its registration number, MH910, was issued in Middlesex in August 1924. Both machines are finished in the colours of the Royal Army Service Corps.

TERRITORIALS OF THE ROYAL ARMY MEDICAL CORPS. Although he has not identified himself, we know that one of these lads is named Archie. In August 1913 he sent this photograph to his mother, Mrs Richardson of 44 Abingdon Road, Southsea: 'Dear Mother, What do you think of your son at camp? Our section have won the challenge cup for night alarm and operations.' The young man standing on the left of the group appears to be a Military Policeman.

BULFORD MILITARY HOSPITAL BEFORE THE FIRST WORLD WAR. The 20th Company, Royal Army Medical Corps had moved to Bulford before January 1904. By April the Station Hospital, as it was known, had been fitted out with 200 beds. In 1917 a much larger Australian hospital had also been built here.

'KOOKS KOSY KORNER', 1909. This postcard from Private R.Y. Green was sent to Miss E. Harris of Park Villas, Station Road, Okehampton, Devon. 'Dear E, What you see on the picture side is our kitchen. When we are on the march we don't even get the overhead shelter. We march off tomorrow 6.30a.m., then my address will be No. 7 Company, attached to 8th Infantry Brigade, 3rd Division, on manoeuvres.' Kitchen hygiene did not seem to concern the boys too much – the young man seated to the left is pouring himself a glass of beer and he has a cigarette in his mouth. The soldier standing third from right appears to be holding a dog – possibly their regimental mascot.

THE FUNERAL OF CAPTAIN EUSTACE BROKE LORAINE. The entourage can be seen passing through Bulford Camp on 8 July 1912. The coffin was being taken to the railway station for onward carriage to Bramford, near Ipswich, and then by road to Captain Loraine's home. A band played Chopin's Funeral March throughout the journey from the camp to the station. A squadron of cavalry, one brigade of the Royal Field Artillery (dismounted), two field companies of the Royal Engineers and one company of the Army Service Corps (dismounted) formed the escort. Captain Loraine, of the Grenadier Guards, and Staff-Sergeant Richard Wilson, of the Royal Engineers, were the first members of the Royal Flying Corps to lose their lives while on flying duty. A photograph of their memorial is reproduced on page 98.

Opposite: THE BULFORD PALLADIUM. The cinema stood at the junction of Marlborough Road and Rawlinson Road between the old riding school and the Gordon Club. At the time of this picture the seat prices were 3d, 6d and 1/-. The programme was changed every Monday, Wednesday and Friday night. The posters that can be seen here are promoting future features which include 'Every Inch a King', 'A Page From Life' and Keystone Comedies. The cinema was demolished before 1939 and a new movie house was built on the site.

AN ARMY SERVICE CORPS FIELD WORKSHOP AT BULFORD IN JULY 1912. The photograph records the transition of 64 Company ASC from a Horse Transport unit to a mechanical one. The mobile machinery workshop appears to be fitted out with a lathe, a stationary engine and a work bench. The unit would seem to be flanked by a pair of Burrell Gold Medal 5-ton steam tractors (No. 3191 supplied W.D. Aldershot, 28 April 1910, and No. 3194 supplied W.D. Bulford, 1 June 1910). On this day the unit received its first motor trucks – three Leylands with Wiltshire registration numbers: AM2262, 2263 and 2264, and three with Hampshire numbers: AA2403, 2406 and 2407.

A WOLSELEY 3-TON ARMY TRUCK AT BULFORD, FEBRUARY 1916. General service and cargo trucks of this type were used in large numbers. They were supplied by numerous British and foreign commercial vehicle manufacturers. The Wolseley, however, was quite rare. A total of only 385 was produced between 1914 and 1918, of which 353 were still in service in the UK at the end of the First World War. The ASC at Bulford are believed to have operated fewer than twenty of them. The one shown here with soldiers Bramhill, Armstege and Brooks was issued with the military registration number, BUL8487.

Opposite: ARMY SERVICE CORPS MECHANICAL TRANSPORT WORKSHOP. A wide range of military vehicles were operated and maintained at Bulford, including ambulances, staff cars, steam tractors and trucks of all sizes. The steam engine shown here appears to be a Fowler double-crank, compound road locomotive of the type used for general haulage and for towing heavy guns and wagons. This particular one served with 63 Company ASC.

THE SHOPS AT DURRINGTON CAMP BEFORE 1916. The development of the army centres on Salisbury Plain gave a great boost to the local communities. Rows of tin and timber clad shops soon began to appear on the main roads running through the camps. At Bulford, Codford, Durrington, Larkhill and Tidworth these shopping parades became known as Tin Towns. The store shown nearest to the camera in this particular picture is that of Deacon and Jay. They were printers, publishers and stationers of Fisherton Street, Salisbury, who later moved to Winchester Street. The neighbouring shop was run by a tobacconist named F.G. Bussell. At the far end of the parade a YMCA hut can just be seen. The delivery van would appear to be a 20 hp Model-T Ford from the pre-First World War era.

A FEW MINUTES OF PEACE AND QUIET. This is the chaplain of the 4th Welsh Brigade, Royal Field Artillery. He appears to be enjoying a quiet smoke and a read outside his tent at Durrington Camp in around 1909. The Army Chaplains' Department, which celebrated its 200th anniversary on 23 September 1996, has provided religious and pastoral support to soldiers whenever needed.

DURHAM LIGHT INFANTRY BLACKSMITHS AT DURRINGTON. We can see that the photograph was taken by Tom Fuller of Amesbury but we have yet to discover the exact location. It would appear to be a farm. The regimental badge of the Durham Light Infantry has been chalked on the anvil. It shows a bugle from which strings extend upwards into the base of a crown. Below it is an inverted horseshoe containing the letters DLI.

A SOLDIER RECEIVES MEDICAL ATTENTION. Personnel of the Royal Army Medical Corps can be seen here giving first-aid to an army officer who has been involved in a minor accident. The exact details are unclear but it would seem that he tripped, fell over and cut his head open while taking part in an military exercise near Durrington in August 1909.

THE ROYAL FLYING CORPS CAMP AT NETHERAVON, 1914. Photographs that show tented accommodation at Netheravon camp are very rare indeed. This is the first such item to have been found by one ardent collector in more than twenty years. Numerous permanent hangars and other buildings were built at Netheravon aerodrome during the winter of 1912-1913, and on 16 June 1913 No. 3 Squadron moved here from Larkhill. A few days later No. 4 Squadron transferred from Farnborough.

A BATHING POOL AT NETHERAVON IN THE TWENTIES. All military personnel were forbidden to swim or bathe in public rivers without first obtaining official permission. In most camps marquees were provided for washing, but there was a limited supply of hot water because of the unavailability of water boilers. To help resolve this problem Southern Command set up a Military Bathing Centre at the Market House (now the Public Library) in Salisbury. Here, men could get a hot bath at set times – subject, of course, to the availability of transport from their camps.

CIVILIAN HUT BUILDERS AT NETHERAVON IN 1913. Some of the original 'black and white' huts that were erected at Lower Airfield Camp can be seen here at the time of their construction. They are single-storey wooden-framed structures set on concrete plinths. The interiors were very basic, incorporating wooden beds with straw mattresses, a few cupboards, a heated stove and two oil lamps. Unfortunately, no one seems able to name the civilian workmen pictured here. They may not have been local men, of course, because hundreds of carpenters, plumbers, electricians and bricklayers came from all over the country to help construct the new camps.

A MID-AIR CRASH AT NETHERAVON, 24 AUGUST 1924. The remains of a Fairey Fawn aircraft are shown here following a mid-air collision in which Leading Aircraftsman Maskell was killed. A Crossley RAF Tender can be seen in the background. Many similar accidents occurred during training flights. The graves of some of the victims can be found in Netheravon churchyard.

A GROUP OF OFFICERS' FIRST SERVANTS. Netheravon has been the home of three outstanding military schools since the beginning of the twentieth century. Thousands of pilots, gunners and cavalry officers have been trained here. This photograph of a very smartly turned out body of men was taken at the Cavalry School on 12 November 1912. A picture of the school building can be seen on the following page.

THE CAVALRY SCHOOL AT NETHERAVON, 1906. The school was established at Netheravon House in 1904, having been acquired by the War Department in March 1898. The house was formerly the residence of Sir Michael Hicks-Beach who was then Chancellor of the Exchequer. An indoor riding school and stables were later built in the grounds. The school was 'closed on mobilisation' at the beginning of the First World War and reopened in October 1919. In 1922 it was transferred to Weedon, Northamptonshire, as part of the School of Equitation. The estate was then taken over as a small arms school.

Opposite: A LEYLAND RAF TENDER AT UPAVON. Registered in Wiltshire in April 1918 (with the mark AM8263), the truck was transferred to RAF Henlow in Hertfordshire in 1921. After the First World War the Leyland company took back many of its trucks and completely refurbished them. The vehicles were then sold to members of the public, some of whom were ex-servicemen. Many new road haulage and charabanc operators started out with one of those ex-War Department vehicles. Some of the firms are still functioning today.

THE FUNERAL OF AN AIRMAN. On 19 March 1914 Lieutenant H.F. Treeby flew out of Netheravon in a Maurice Farman biplane. Coming into land after a twenty minute flight, the aeroplane stalled and fell to the ground. The lieutenant was crushed beneath the body of the plane and killed. This photograph shows his funeral cortege passing through Upavon on 23 March.

FREDDIE MILLS AND FRIENDS AT RAF UPAVON IN 1943. This Second World War group photograph features the former British Heavyweight Boxing Champion. Pictured left to right are Squadron Leader J.S. Holloway (known as 'Stanley'), Station Adjutant Rogers, Sergeant Freddie Mills, Mr F.M. Broadrib, who is believed to have been the boxer's manager, and, on the right, Group Captain A. 'Speedy' Holmes.

Five
Around Tilshead, Shrewton and Larkhill

A SHOW OF STRENGTH AT TILSHEAD IN 1933. These are the fighting machines of the 5th or 6th Battalion, Royal Tank Corps. The heavier vehicles are Medium Mark II battle tanks and the lighter ones are Carden-Loyd carriers. These tiny tracked vehicles were operated by a crew of two; they were equipped with a machine gun and were used primarily for reconnaissance purposes.

A WATER BOWSER AT TILSHEAD CAMP BEFORE THE FIRST WORLD WAR. This would seem to be a Royal Engineers Signals unit. An array of signalling equipment can be seen in the background. The two-wheeled horse-drawn water carrier appears to be fitted with hand-operated pumps which would have been used to fill the tank. It would be discharged by gravity. The badges on the pipe smoker's jacket would suggest that he is a bandsman and stretcher bearer. Why are they wearing their hats back to front?

A RESERVED FORCES CAMP AT TILSHEAD BEFORE 1914. These are the men of C Company, 4th Wilts Territorial Regiment. The picture was set up for Albert Marett, a commercial photographer from Shrewton. It would appear that there was a plentiful supply of food at the camp. Several loaves of bread are stuck on the sharp ends of the rifle bayonets that make up the centrepiece of the picture. There is also a display of tin mugs and plates below the rifles. The soldiers seated in the foreground are holding tent peg mallets.

MOBILISED MEDICS AT WEST DOWN CAMP. The crew of this Type II General Service wagon represent C Company, 3rd London Field Ambulance, of the 1st London Division Territorial Force. One of the lads had thoughtfully scribbled a note on the back of the original photograph: 'Winnie is the horse with the saddle on, and Tommy is the other. Tommy is the most valuable horse we've got, he is worth between £90 & £100.'

THE COMPANY KITCHEN AT WEST DOWN 'NORTH' CAMP. The soldier depicted second from the right is Arthur Ashman, who then lived at 39 Belvedere, Lansdown Road, Bath. He sent this photograph to his wife in August 1908. West Down was one of the first camps on Salisbury Plain, having been created in 1903. A water bowser similar to the one shown on page 82 can be seen on the left.

HAVING FUN WITH A NEW BOY AT BUSTARD CAMP IN 1908. This photograph carries a note that was written for Len Coombes of D Division CTO London EC. 'This shows a few of us having a bit of fun with one of the 'rookies', i.e. new men. This one was particularly susceptible to a bit of 'kid'. Will tell you all about him on Monday. Yours Reg.' We believe that Reg has marked his position at the back of the group with a cross. It is a pity that we will never know what he said to Len about the new boy when they met that following Monday.

CANADIAN EXPEDITIONARY FORCES ARRIVE ON SALISBURY PLAIN, 1914. In October camps were prepared at Bustard, West Down (North and South) and Pond Farm. More than 33,000 men were trained here before leaving for the battlefields of France. The wet weather conditions throughout the winter of 1914-1915 were the worst in living memory. Thousands of soldiers were taken ill with influenza and other similar illnesses. Many of them died and were buried in cemeteries and churchyards across South Wiltshire.

A CANADIAN SIGNALS UNIT AT POND FARM. Taken in November 1914, this photograph shows the signallers of 2nd Battalion, 1st Infantry Brigade of the Canadian Expeditionary Force. A heliograph, semaphore flags and signalling lamps can all be seen here.

CORPORAL A.N. NASH served with the 1st Canadian Regiment. The words on the back of his photograph tell a sad story: 'A Walkerville, Toronto, Midland and Detroit Bum. Caught by military Fisher one day and found in uniform the next. Got hit on the dome on June 15th, 1915 at Givenchy.'

CANADIANS IN THE FLOOD AT SHREWTON, JANUARY 1915. The picture clearly depicts the scene in Elston Lane. Many Canadians were billeted in Shrewton and other neighbouring villages at the time because of the appalling conditions in the tented camps. Between October 1914 and February 1915, rain fell on 89 of the 123 days. Temperatures dropped below freezing and, combined with high winds, this made life extremely uncomfortable for the soldiers.

KING GEORGE V INSPECTS THE CANADIAN EXPEDITIONARY FORCE.
Accompanied by Lord Kitchener, who was then Secretary of State for War, the King inspected
the Canadians on two separate occasions. The first event was arranged for November 1914,
soon after their arrival, and the second visit took place on 4 February 1915, shortly before the
men left for France. Here we can see an artillery unit passing the saluting base. In the
background one can also just make out the massed ranks of foot soldiers. The spectators had
arrived in cars, on horse back and in horse-drawn carriages.

THE 'K' BATTERY KITCHEN AT ROLLESTONE CAMP IN 1911. These men of the Royal Horse Artillery were photographed by Tom Fuller. It would seem that they are members of a firewood picquet. The soldier seen lounging here in the right foreground is believed to be Bert Tredwell.

A TEA BREAK FOR THE CIVILIAN HUT BUILDERS AT ROLLESTONE CAMP, 1914. General labourers and men with specialist skills were brought in from all over Great Britain to erect the huts at Rollestone and other Salisbury Plain camps. The War Department had hoped to have all the troops properly accommodated in huts by the end of November 1914 but, even with the assistance of 900 Canadians, mainly bricklayers and carpenters, there were still 11,000 men sleeping under canvas at Christmas.

A FIELD INSPECTION BY LORD KITCHENER, JULY 1915. Then Secretary of State for War, Lord Kitchener is the more distant of the two officers standing in the middle of the picture. On 5 June the following year he was lost at sea when the armoured cruiser HMS *Hampshire* struck a German mine and sank off the Orkneys. There were no survivors.

CONTRACTORS TO THE MILITARY. The Salisbury firm of Wort and Way were fortunate to be granted numerous Government contracts at the time of the First World War. Their workmen built many of the huts at Rollestone Camp, which is where this picture of one of their heavy horse wagons was taken. This wooden-framed hut is clad with corrugated iron.

FARGO CAMP AT THE TIME OF THE FIRST WORLD WAR. This camp was situated between the Packway at Larkhill and the northern end of Fargo Plantation. By 1915 many huts had already been erected in and around Larkhill – replacing tents such as the ones that can be seen here at Fargo. Messrs Wort and Way and Sir John Jackson were among the more prominent contractors working in this area. The white huts that can just be made out on the skyline are part of Fargo Hospital. About a hundred of the New Zealand and Australian soldiers who died at the Fargo and Tidworth hospitals were buried in Tidworth Cemetery. The large dark coloured building that comes into view in the background on the left of the picture was put up in 1905. It can still be seen today.

THE COMPANY MASCOT. This horse was the lucky talisman of D Company, 4H/37 RBH, who were encamped at Hamilton in 1914. The animal would seem to be wearing a pair of trousers on its front legs, a soldier's hat on its head, and a bandoleer around its neck. Named after General Sir Ian Hamilton, the encampment was to be found opposite Fargo Camp.

A MOTHER AND CHILD AT LARKHILL IN 1914. This delightful photograph was taken by Tom Fuller on 1 June. The colt had just been born at a Royal Horse Artillery territorial camp at Larkhill. The army treasured their horses – they have been described as the greatest single factor contributing to the effectiveness of the army. They were essential to every aspect of military activity before the First World War.

A MONKEY PUZZLE. This monkey was the mascot of one particular battery of Royal Field Artillery at Larkhill. The original owner of the photograph could not remember which: 'It was the 74th or the 79th Battery; they were both here.' Notice the cannon motif on the monkey's upper arm. It is also holding a swagger stick. Many companies kept a mascot, but this one is very unusual.

LONDON ARTILLERY MEN AT LARKHILL, 1913. These are the men of Sub-Section C of the 1st London Company, Royal Field Artillery. One of the individuals pictured here wrote a note on the back of the original photograph: 'Some of the boys are waiting for dinner, hungry as bears.' The battery bugler is the young man seated on the bucket in the middle of the group.

ROYAL HORSE ARTILLERY LIMBER GUNNERS AT LARKHILL, 1913. The War Office purchased land at Larkhill and West Down in the late 1890s. At first, during the summer months only, the centres were used as territorial training camps. Very few permanent buildings were put up before the First World War. The members of this team were being trained to operate a 13-pounder field gun.

PUTTING IN THE FINISHING TOUCHES AT LARKHILL IN 1915. The soldiers themselves were asked to construct the paths and roads that ran through the camps. The appalling weather that prevailed from October 1914 to February 1915 meant the contractors were well behind schedule. The photograph on the opposite page clearly shows the terrible ground conditions at that time.

Opposite: BOGGED DOWN AT LARKHILL, JANUARY 1915. This is not a river that we can see here, but a road. It would be typical of any scene in the central area of Salisbury Plain at that time. The horse-drawn cart does not appear to be a military vehicle. It is probably one of the wagons used by the firm Wort and Way (Government contractors and builders) of 37 and 180 Castle Street, Salisbury. One can see how similar it looks to the cart that is shown on page 89. The steam engine is a Fowler double-crank, road locomotive weighing about 16 tons (16, 250 kg). It is of the type used to tow heavy guns and wagons. Although we cannot see what is going on behind the machine, one can imagine that it is being used to pull out a vehicle which has become stuck in the mud.

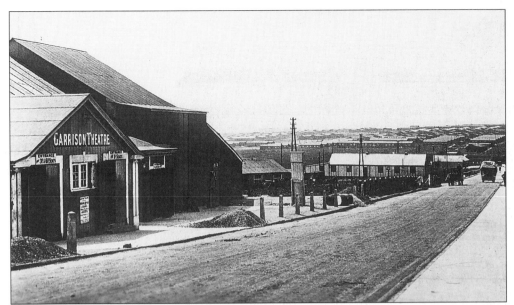

THE MAIN ROAD AND NUMBER 20 CAMP, LARKHILL, IN THE TWENTIES. This is a western view of what is now known as The Packway. The Military Cinema was built in 1915, on the north side of the main road. It was destroyed by fire four years later and replaced by The Garrison Theatre, shown on the left of this picture. The patrons who chose to sit in the 3d and 6d seats would enter the auditorium through the door on the left. Access to the 1s seats was gained through the right door. One can just see that the fields in the distance are covered with row upon row of wooden and iron-clad huts.

'COLONEL' CODY AT LARKHILL, AUGUST 1912. Samuel Franklin Cody was an American aviator and an inventor who became a British subject in 1909. Shortly before this photograph was taken he had received first prize and an order for two of his flying machines following his success at the Larkhill Military Trials. Cody was not a real Colonel – it appears that King George V had once inadvertently called him 'Colonel Cody' and the title seemed to stick. He was tragically killed on 7 August 1913 while flying over Laffan's Plain, Farnborough.

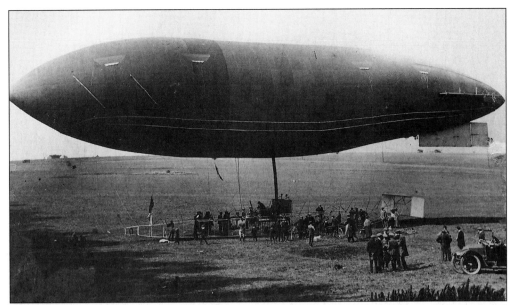

THE ARMY AIRSHIP *GAMMA 1* ON SALISBURY PLAIN, 1912. The craft had arrived from Farnborough on 22 September with six passengers. The Beta and Gamma airships were frequent visitors to South Wiltshire. The Air Battalion RE was formed in 1911 with its headquarters in Farnborough. No. 1 Company was responsible for airships, balloons and kites. No. 2 Company, based at Larkhill, was associated with fixed wing aircraft. It seems clear from this photograph that airships would create a great deal of interest wherever they went.

THE AVRO G-TYPE 60 HORSE POWER BIPLANE AT LARKHILL AERODROME, 1912. This is a scene from the War Office aeroplane trials that took place at Larkhill from 1-25 August. Twenty-four machines were tested. Each one had to comply with a number of requirements relating to its take off, landing, payload and endurance. Here we can see some riggers at work fitting up the wire stays that separate the wings.

AN AIR DISASTER, FRIDAY 5 JULY 1912. The sheet of canvas hides the wreckage of a Nieuport monoplane that was being flown by Captain Eustace Loraine and Staff-Sergeant Richard Wilson. At about 5.40a.m. the aeroplane began a steep turn approximately one and a half miles west of Stonehenge and at a height of about 400 ft. In the middle of the turn the nose of the monoplane dropped sharply and it dived into the ground. Both occupants were killed.

THE INAUGURATION OF THE MEMORIAL AT AIRMAN'S CROSS, 5 JULY 1913. A year to the day after the accident this memorial was unveiled at the junction of the Salisbury and Devizes Roads. Carved from Cornish granite, the monument has the appearance of an eighth-century cross. It bears the following inscription: 'To the Memory of Captain Loraine and Staff-Sergeant Wilson, Who whilst flying on duty met with an accident near this spot on July 5th 1912.' After years of neglect the memorial has now been restored. The compilers of this book were privileged to be present at the rededication ceremony which took place on Friday 5 July 1996. A photograph of Captain Loraine's funeral procession can be seen on page 69.

MAJOR 'A.J.' HEWETSON RFA.
An officer of the 66th Battery Royal
Field Artillery, he was killed when
out taking a test for his aviator's
certificate. On 17 July 1913 the
Bristol Prier monoplane in which he
was flying crashed near Larkhill
aerodrome. A memorial cross was
dedicated to his memory. Carved by
Arthur and Jack Green of Tisbury
Stone Quarries, it can still be seen in
the south-east corner of Fargo
Plantation, a few minutes walk from
Stonehenge on the north side of the
Devizes road.

THE WRECKED MONOPLANE IN WHICH MAJOR HEWETSON WAS KILLED.

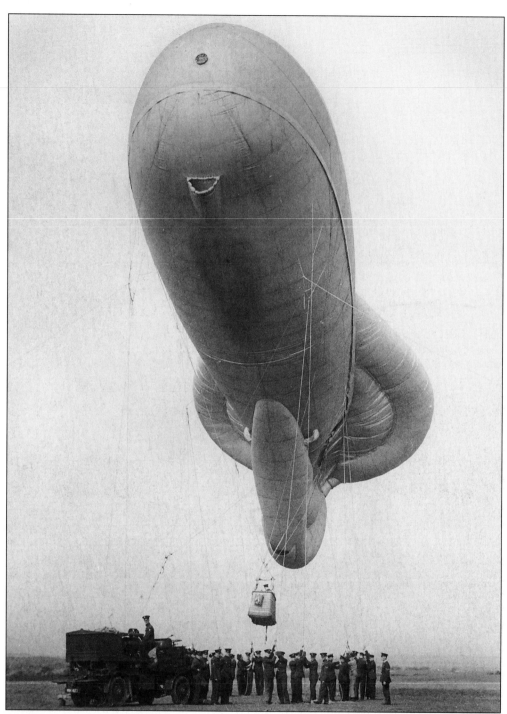

AN FWD BALLOON WINCH AT LARKHILL IN THE THIRTIES. From very early on the army used spotter planes and balloons to help improve the accuracy of the artillery guns. The Royal Flying Corps had taken over fifty acres of land on the west side of the Bustard road and the No. 1 Balloon School was established there. Two of the original hangars can still be seen on the site.

Six

Around Warminster, Sutton Veny, Codford and Fovant

A MILITARY SCENE AT WARMINSTER IN 1915. The First World War transformed Warminster from a small Wiltshire market town to a bustling military centre. A large body of men from the Devon Regiment can be seen here as they march past the fountain. The corps of drums take the lead, followed by the band. Also shown are a number of soldiers who joined the townspeople in the Market Place to watch the passing troops.

MEDICS ON MANOEUVRES BEFORE THE FIRST WORLD WAR. Voluntary troops have been in existence at Warminster since the Napoleonic invasion threat. After the Great War of 1914-1918, greater numbers of soldiers were concentrated in the area. There was a very large Army Service Corps depot in Station Road. This photograph shows members of 6th Field Ambulance at a summer training camp on the outskirts of the town. General Service wagons and bell tents are seen in the background.

ARMY ORDNANCE CORPS FOOTBALL TEAM, 1917-18. Their normal role was to supply the army with stores and equipment.

OFF TO THE WHITE HART FOR A DRINK! It would seem that the six soldiers pictured here in the comfort of this 20 hp Model-T Ford hackney cab are about to leave camp at Warminster for an evening on the town. Their host, Elan James Wickham, was the licensee of the White Hart public house in George Street. He appears to have been an astute businessman for he was also the licensed operator of this taxi (AM5095) which he had acquired in June 1915. Four years later he had sold it to Mrs Emily Grist of Sweetland Cottage, Bishopstrow.

SANDHILL CAMP AT LONGBRIDGE DEVERILL DURING THE GREAT WAR. There were ten huts in this row, of which numbers three to seven are shown. Vast amounts of timber and other materials were needed to build the camps around Warminster. Much of it was carried on the Sutton Veny Camp Railway which ran from Heytesbury station to Longbridge Deverill. There is an air of informality about this particular picture: the soldiers look quite at ease and have clothes hung out on lines in front of their huts.

TURNING OUT BREAD NEAR LONGBRIDGE DEVERILL IN AROUND 1916. Here we can see a field section at work. Freshly baked bread is being removed from ovens that have been constructed in a field. The tin loaves are very large indeed, measuring approximately 24 inches square. The chalked caption on the oven door in the left foreground informs us that these are the men of No. 4 Section, 65th Field Bakery, Army Service Corps.

A CAMP IN THE MAKING AT SUTTON VENY, 1915. This is a view of some of the huts that were erected in a field to the north of Five Ash Lane. It would appear that they are constructed entirely of wood. Many of the huts built on the central and northern encampments of Salisbury Plain stood on brick piers or concrete bases, and some were clad with sheets of corrugated iron. One can just see a light railway track running through the centre of the site. This would have been used for bringing in supplies of timber. At the end of the First World War many of the huts were sold to local parish councils. They had many uses, such as village halls, chapels, class rooms and workshops. A number of them are known to be still in use.

Opposite: LOCAL BOYS MARCHING THROUGH SUTTON VENY IN AUGUST 1915. These soldiers from the 7th Wiltshire Regiment are marching briskly along the village High Street. The quiet communities of the Wylye Valley soon became used to such scenes. Many people opened their homes to the soldiers as a welcome change from the Spartan conditions they had to endure in camp.

PONGO AT SUTTON VENY, the mascot of the 7th Wiltshire Regiment. The photograph was taken by camp photographer, Mr S.J. Vowles. He would have sold thousands of photographic postcards during the years of the Great War. His pictures can still be found in junk shops, antique markets and at collectors' fairs. Good examples of his work can be purchased for just a few pounds. A number of them are to be seen in this book.

SPECIALIST SOLDIERS AT HEYTESBURY, JANUARY 1917. These men are dressed for action – they are all wearing tin helmets. The soldier seated on the extreme right of the second row is also wearing body armour. His was a front-line role perhaps? It would seem, then, that these are the members of an explosives unit or a demolition squad.

A BUSY SCENE AT CORTON CAMP AT THE TIME OF THE FIRST WORLD WAR. The development of the Codford area as a military centre, like many others, was largely dependent on a railway connection. Smoke from a train on the Great Western line can be seen in the distance. This was linked to the Codford line further east. The camp stable blocks come into view on the right of the photograph, and there is also one block shown on the left (nearest to the camera). The administration and accommodation buildings would seem to be those seen in the background. One small hut appears to be the telecommunications point – it has a telegraph pole and wires attached to it. At the moment this picture was taken, many of the horses were feeding from the troughs.

THE NEW CODFORD CAMP MOTOR FIRE ENGINE. Pictured here outside the camp fire station is a Merryweather 3-ton petrol-driven fire engine – AM8940. It was registered in Wiltshire on 28 October 1918. The Secretary of State for War, at the War Office in London, provided the vehicle for government use at Codford camp. The machine has wooden artillery wheels fitted with solid rubber tyres. The drive to the rear wheels would seem to be by chains. A short extension ladder is carried; also a first-aid hose reel which is located in a central position. A Merryweather 'Hatfield' water pump with vertical air vessel is mounted at the back of the appliance. It was taken out of service on 21 February 1923. The soldiers pictured here would appear to be from several regiments.

Opposite: THE CODFORD CAMP RAILWAY, BUILT IN 1914. On leaving Codford station, the Codford Military Railway curved eastwards to cross the main road north-west of Codford St Peter church. It continued westward through Camp 15 to cross the road from Codford St Peter to Manor Farm from whence it curved and headed due east through Camps 13 and 14. At this point the line divided. The original track continued on to end north-west of Codford Hill. The branch ran southwards, passing to the east of Codford St Mary before terminating at Camp 5. Here we can see Camp No. 6. The Sergeants' Mess is shown on the left. The Guard House is on the right and the Cook House comes into view in the distance.

SALISBURY ROAD, CODFORD, BEFORE 1920. This is a scene at No. 4 Camp, which was situated east of the village near a place called Foxhole Bottom on the Salisbury to Shaftesbury road (A30). It was occupied by the men of the 25th Division. The 26th Division had been allocated sites at Sherrington, Boyton, Upton Lovell and Corton. By the end of the First World War fifteen camps had been created in and around Codford.

SOME CANTERBURY BOYS AT CODFORD. In July 1916 Codford Camp had been chosen as the New Zealand Command Depot. Here are the words of one of their countrymen, seen in this picture of the inside of Hut 5. 'Dear Grandfather. I am going up for medical exam this week. I think I shall be marked 'A' this time. If so, my stay in England will not be long. A big draft is going away from here to-morrow for the front. Give my love to Freddie and all. Your affectionate grandson, Arthur.'

MERE CAMP, AUGUST 1908. This appears to be a summer training camp for the territorial soldiers of the Wiltshire Regiment. The covered horse-drawn wagon appears to be owned by Chaplin and Co, a firm that carried parcels for the railway companies. Their vehicles were once a common sight right across the country. We can imagine that a shopkeeper or the army had hired this cart from one of their Wiltshire offices. It possibly came from the Amesbury branch (see also page 14) which was managed by Mr A.S. Asher. It could also have been hired from the Salisbury office, that was to be found at 12 Milford Street (manager George Emery of 16 Woodstock Road). Whoever it was using the vehicle, they were sure to have been made welcome by the soldiers. There are all kinds of good things on sale here including several varieties of Peek Frean biscuits.

Opposite: 'MY LITTLE WOODEN HUT'. An ironic message on a card signed simply 'Wallace' and dated 1 October 1916. The postcard picture shows a small contingent of men and two General Service wagons near huts 31 and 32 at Camp No. 6 in Codford. Soldiers were often sent here after enjoying fourteen days convalescent leave. This, and the fact that they had to contend constantly with mud and lice, did not enhance the camp's popularity.

A VAD HOSPITAL AT TISBURY VICARAGE, OCTOBER 1916. The Revd F.E. Hutch-inson generously handed over the keys to his home at the beginning of the Great War. It was put to good use as a hospital for wounded soldiers. The staff were members of a Voluntary Aid Detachment that was set up by Mrs Walter Shaw-Stewart of Fonthill Abbey. Before the hospital at Fovant Camp was opened in 1915, operations were performed here.

'HOSPITAL BLUES', a common name for the uniform worn by soldiers in hospital. The jacket is coloured blue, the tie red and the shirt white. The men pictured here were being nursed at a Voluntary Aid Detachment hospital in Mere in around 1916. The Scottish soldier on the extreme right of the group is wearing a soft head dress known as a 'Tam-o-Shanter'.

MEDIUM MARK II TANKS PASSING THROUGH MERE IN 1928. The battle tanks shown here are part of a large army of fighting machines en route to Taunton during a mechanised warfare exercise planned by Southern Command. The leading tank (T64) carries 2nd Lieutenant Harding-Newman of A Company, 5th Battalion Royal Tank Corps. The driver of the Morris saloon appears to have pulled over to allow the noisy tracked vehicles to pass by in safety. His car has a Coventry registration number, VB1170.

FOVANT CAMP AT THE TIME OF THE GREAT WAR. For some unknown reason photographs of this camp are very rare. The answer may lie in the fact that there has never been a resident photographer in the area. This rather dull view shows the huts that were built in the fields between the Salisbury to Shaftesbury Road and the London and South Western Railway line. Some of the soldiers who were stationed here at the time of the First World War had carved the badges of their regiments into the chalk down land. These are now a popular tourist attraction.

THE FOVANT GARRISON CINEMA. Shops, restaurants, a bank and a cinema grew up around the camp. The Garrison Cinema was to be found in Green Drove. It was a particularly popular place where all the latest films could be seen. The large wooden notice board tells us that the cinema was run under the direction of the Navy and Army Canteen Company. Performances were held 'Twice Nightly' and 'Only First Class Pictures and Programmes' were shown. Admission prices were 3d and 6d, or 1s if a seat was reserved. When the cinema was demolished some years ago, a bungalow was built on the site. The entrance steps complete with flanking brick walls and urns were retained. They can still be seen.

Opposite: A PHOTO OPPORTUNITY AT THE FOVANT YMCA. The rapid expansion of the army at the start of the First World War led to an urgent need for recreation and canteen facilities for the troops. The YMCA was one of the first institutions to respond. A unit such as the one shown here would have been found in almost every camp in the country. This particular one is believed to be the 'Reading and Writing' hut built at Fovant Camp.

THE ENTRANCE TO HURDCOTT CAMP, JULY 1916. The badge of the Finsbury Rifles was to be seen at the eastern end of the Fovant encampment. Situated close to Barford St Martin, the emblem incorporates the motto 'Pro Aris Et Focis' (For our Altar and our Homes). In March 1917 Hurdcott House became the headquarters of No. 3 Command Depot of the Australian Imperial Force. It had previously been occupied by other Colonial troops, some of whom were recovering from the wounds of war.

ARMY SERVICE CORPS TRANSPORT AT HURDCOTT IN AROUND 1916. The soldiers would seem to be wearing the uniforms of a Gloucester regiment. An inscription that can be seen on the frame of the cart shows that it was made by Vincent & Company of Reading. For many years they had a reputation for turning out well-made bodies for horse-drawn and motorised military vehicles.

Seven
The Photographs of Austin Underwood
The 1960s

A BUSY SUMMER WEEKEND IN AMESBURY. Being on the main route from London to the West Country, traffic congestion in Amesbury was getting progressively worse. A by-pass was desperately needed and Austin Underwood was among several individuals who spearheaded a long campaign for a road to be constructed away from the town. This photograph depicts a typical scene in Countess Road in the early 1960s. Nearest to the camera is a 'Black and White' coach from the Associated Motorways fleet heading for Liverpool by way of Cheltenham Spa.

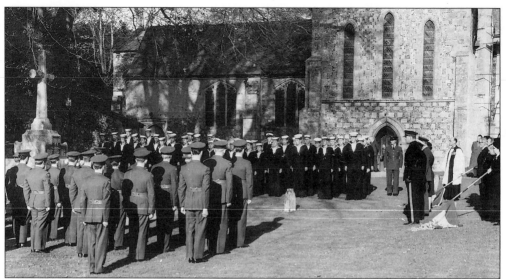

THE RE-DEDICATION OF AMESBURY WAR MEMORIAL, 1964. Originally situated near the chestnut tree in the centre of the town, it was re-positioned in the churchyard of the parish church of St Mary and St Melor. The picture shows representatives of the Royal Air Force, the Royal Navy and the British Legion who attended the service of re-consecration. An army officer in dress uniform can also be seen. The Revd Geoffrey Hazelton officiated.

NUCLEAR WAR GAMES AT IMBER. During the late 1950s and early 1960s several Civil Defence exercises took place on Salisbury Plain. The individuals pictured here are members of a Mobile Rescue Unit from Southampton. They are equipped with ropes, ladders, a stretcher, trenching spades, axes and first aid dressings. A number of Wiltshire boy scouts volunteered to act as casualties. Peter Daniels, co-author of this book, was among them. Being a scout from the 10th Salisbury troop, he was carefully buried under brick rubble before being extracted by a Civil Defence unit. Theatrical make-up was used to create some very realistic looking wounds on the bodies, heads and limbs of the casualties.

THE BIG FREEZE OF SIXTY-THREE. In the early part of the year, frost, snow and high winds created havoc across the country. Thick snow covered South Wiltshire with drifts in some places averaging five feet. The A345 between Amesbury and Salisbury was described as 'a snow-walled gully with the occasional buried car'. A yellow Wiltshire County Council tractor (RMR993) can be seen here alongside a tracked crawler fitted with a bulldozer attachment.

THE FUNERAL OF BERT FELLENDER, 1963. Mr Fellender lived in Salisbury Street, Amesbury, and for many years he was employed by the Antrobus family as their chauffeur. For forty-two years he was a member of the British Legion Club and one of his former colleagues, Albert Goodhugh, can be seen here carrying the British Legion banner at the front of the funeral procession. The Revd Geoffrey Hazelton walks ahead of the Austin hearse as it proceeds very slowly across Queensberry Bridge.

AMESBURY CARNIVAL CAPERS, 1966. This float was organised by the National Association of Youth Clubs. The annual carnival has been a fixture in the Amesbury calendar for very many years although its popularity has waxed and waned. Formerly held in the grounds of Amesbury Abbey, in more recent times the venue has been the Recreation Fields. Usually arranged to take place on the nearest Saturday to the Summer Solstice, the proceeds are donated to deserving local causes.

THE END OF AN ERA. On 22 June 1911 Sir Edmund Antrobus planted a young horse chestnut tree in the centre of Amesbury to commemorate the coronation of King George V. In 1964 the mature tree was uprooted by Wiltshire County Council employees instructed to clear a path for the A345 road that was to be permanently diverted through the grounds of Amesbury House. There was strong opposition from both the Amesbury Rural District Council and the Parish Council. Austin Underwood believed that if any single event marked the transition of Amesbury from a village to a town then this was it. The photograph above is one of the last taken of this magnificent tree. The Plaza Cinema and the Co-operative building can be seen in the background.

Opposite: Austin Underwood's daughters, Judith and Ruth, were among several children who collected leaves from the hose chestnut as souvenirs. Throughout the fifty-three years of its existence the tree had provided a source of shade for older residents and of supply of conkers for the younger generations. The base of the War Memorial in its original position is shown on the right of the picture.

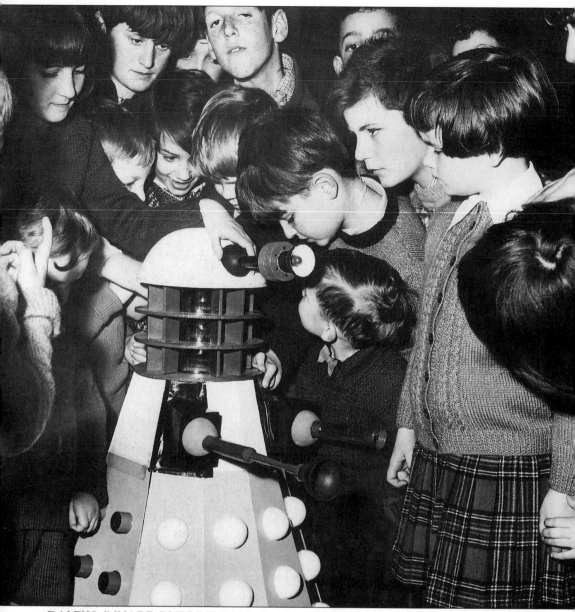

DALEKS INVADE DURRINGTON. A fully automated alien from the popular *Dr Who* television series fascinated the youngsters who were fortunate enough to attend the Durrington Labour Party children's party in 1965. The robot from outer space moved among them by remote control. The party had been arranged for an earlier date but was postponed because of a by-election.

Opposite: THE BULFORD PRAM RACE, 1966. Held traditionally on Boxing Day, this annual affair became known as 'The Idiots' Race'. It was a popular event in the 1960s, attracting teams from a wide area. The contenders who were first to successfully cross the River Avon were declared the winners. The incumbent of the pram was always expected to be dressed as a baby. On this particular occasion there appears to be lot of cheating going on, but it was all in good spirits.

THE AMESBURY OLD AGE PENSIONERS' TEA PARTY. Members of the Amesbury Friendship Club held monthly meetings at the Methodist Church Hall in High Street. The picture above shows some of the women who helped serve tea at the party held on 15 May 1965. Left to right are Flo Chilcott, Elsie Pennels, Joan Newman, Mrs Clarke, Gwen Aust, Winnie Kett, Gwen Jenkins, Iris Retter, Mrs Earnshaw and Dorothy Cooper.

CHURN ROLLING IN SALISBURY STREET, 1966, one of several entertainments that took place before the start of the annual Amesbury Carnival Parade. The area shown in this photograph was formerly the town market place, the thoroughfare being approximately twice its present width and with a tree-lined centre. The Bell Hotel (previously The Swan) was rebuilt after a disastrous fire in 1908.

Opposite: THE GREAT STONEHENGE BOGLE MYSTERY, 1966. On 17 February the custodian at Stonehenge, George Smith, arrived to see an astonishing sight. During the night the stones had been decorated with huge cut-out hardboard figures. There were sixteen in number, all of them wearing Beatles hairstyles and measuring approximately seven feet in height. They were suspended over the stones with weighted cords and each one wielded a hammer. Known collectively as the Bogles, their names all began with the letter 'B'. Here we can see Bob, Bruce and Bud. The perpetrators of this brilliant hoax have never been discovered. Several of the Bogles are now living in a private garage in Amesbury.

THE AMESBURY ROMAN CATHOLIC FETE QUEEN AND HER ATTENDANTS, 1966.
Sixteen-year-old Daphne Billington is pictured here with her sister Dianne, aged 20, and Janis
Muirhead (right) who was 17. They were chosen at a special Fete Dance at which the London
pop group, The Equators, played. The band leader Elton Grant was one of the judges.

THE DEMOLITION OF THE AMESBURY UNION WORKHOUSE, 1967. Built by Gilbert Scott in 1836, the workhouse was a prominent landmark on the southern edge of the town. It catered for the homeless and needy across a wide area of Salisbury Plain. It ceased to function as a workhouse in the 1950s and became a factory and a warehouse. Numerous private houses occupy the site today. The last Workhouse Master was Robert Bence, who died in December 1995, a month before his old home was demolished.

THE BONNY BABY COMPETITORS AT DURRINGTON CHURCH FETE, 1968. Sitting third and fourth from the left are Monica Edwards with Paula and Wendy Bird with Nigel. Paula has just produced a bonny baby of her own. The Fete Queen and her entourage can be seen in the back row. Where are they now?

SUNRISE AT STONEHENGE, 1969. Even before the arrival of the 'New Age' travellers many people came to witness the Druidical solstice ceremonies. On this particular occasion a young man climbed to the top of one of the tallest trilithons where he stripped to his underwear just before the Druids entered the inner circle. In earlier times the entertainment had been provided by the Amesbury Town Band.

A NEW ROAD AT LAST! The long-awaited opening on the 5 September 1969 of the Amesbury By-pass. Mrs Lush, her daughter Kath, Steve Penny and Horace Purchase stand among the group of spectators on the right. Harold Eyres can also be seen. His family ran the Amesbury carrier service for very many years. In the background is the Iron Age site known as Vespasian's Camp.

Acknowledgements

The enjoyment that Rex and I have experienced while compiling this book has been greatly enhanced by the enthusiasm of the many people whom we have approached during the course of our research. The success of a collection of photographs such as this depends very much on several factors. The quality and quantity of suitable material and the generosity of the public. We have been fortunate in all ways. The number of historical photographs that have survived on Salisbury Plain has surprised both of us and we have grown to appreciate the kindness of its people more than ever.

We are particularly grateful to Mrs Mary Underwood for giving us unlimited access to her late husband's photographs: The Austin Underwood Collection. To Mr Norman Parker who kindly checked the accuracy of the captions and to Mr David Fletcher (Librarian, The Tank Museum, Bovington), Mr Peter Goodhugh and Mrs Betty Hooper for the historical information they have provided.

We would also like to thank the following individuals and organisations who have helped in many different ways: Harry Foot (Librarian, Army Air Museum, Middle Wallop); Terry Clark (Army Public Relations Office, H.Q. 3rd (UK) Division, Bulford Camp); The Achivist 9/12th Lancers, Derby Museum; Peter Carey (Imber Land Warden); Lynne and David Perkins of Kallans Photography; Angela Turnbull (Features Editor, Salisbury Journal); Judith Giles and Bruce Purvis (Librarians, Salisbury Local Studies Library); Members of the Salisbury Militaria Society; Graham Chadwick (Secretary, The Brockhurst Artillery): Roger Davies and Tony Pridmore of The Royal Armouries, Fort Nelson; The staff at Wiltshire Record Office, Trowbridge; Alan Alexander, Molly Archer-Smith, Julian Beacham, Joy Brockington, Len Campbell, Chris David, Frances Dean, Monica Edwards, Ted and Betsie Green, Terry Heffernan, Mary Holloway, Richard Larden, Taffy Leach, Michael Maidment, Air Vice Marshall B. H. Newton (Retired), Peter Parrish, Tony Pickernell, Iris Retter and friends, Rex and Helen Reynolds, Christine Richardson, Roy Simper and John Woods.

Peter R Daniels
Netherhampton
October 1996